Hiii!

Thank you so much for buying my book!
Before starting your coloring journey, please read:

Paper Quality

Amazon's paper is ideal for coloring with colored pencils and alcohol-based markers. To prevent bleed-through and protect the next page, place a blank sheet of thicker paper behind the page you are coloring.

Share your creations!

I would love to see your artwork. Please feel free to share your creations with me on TikTok at @jeanettveronicaart or on Instagram @jeanettveronicacoloringbooks

Newsletter!

Sign up for free monthly coloring pages at https://boldandeasy.jeanettveronicacoloring.com

Connect with me!

Any questions or concerns? Reach out at info@jeanettveronicacoloring.com

THIS COLORING BOOK BELONGS TO

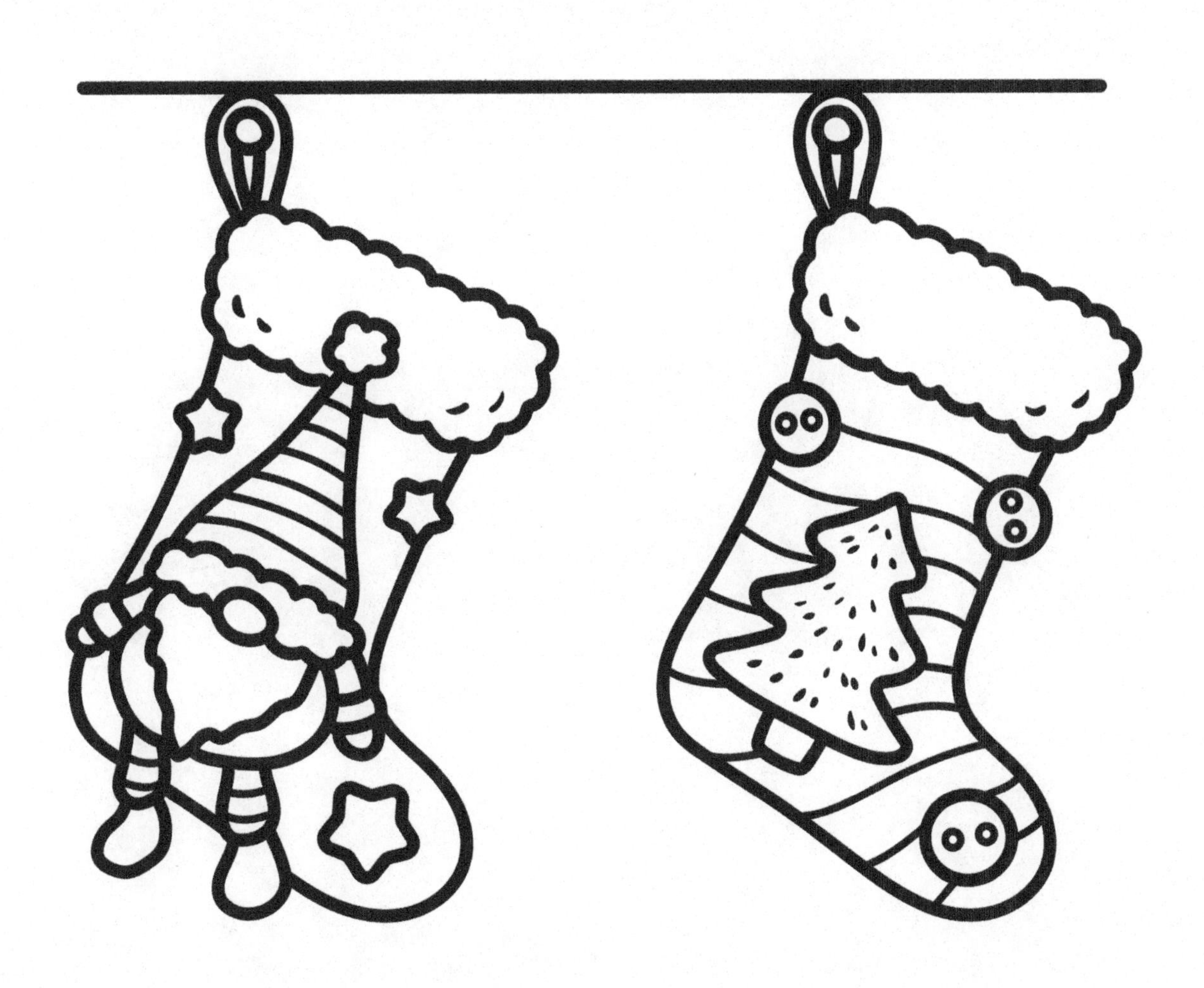

COLOR TEST PAGE

Just a GIRL
who LOVES
CHRISTMAS!

I love
Coffee...

Sweet
Merry
Christmas

Cozy
Winter
Vibe

Merry
Christmas

Merry
Christmas

HO HO HO!

HO HO HO

BOOKSTORE

Santa

Cherry Pink
Dark Green

Made in the USA
Monee, IL
16 December 2024